BREAD
AND OTHER
MIRACLES

BREAD
AND OTHER
MIRACLES

LYNN UNGAR

authorHOUSE®

AuthorHouse™
1663 Liberty Drive
Bloomington, IN 47403
www.authorhouse.com
Phone: 1-800-839-8640

Published by AuthorHouse   10/04/2012

ISBN: 978-1-4772-7358-6 (sc)
ISBN: 978-1-4772-7359-3 (e)

Library of Congress Control Number: 2012917773

For Kelsey—these poems still belong to you.

Contents

Part 1

Blessing the Bread

Blessing the Bread

Baruch atah Adonai, Eloheinu melech ha'olam,
hamotzi lechem min ha'aretz.

Surely the earth
is heavy with this rhythm,
the stretch and pull of bread,
the folding in and folding in
across the palms, as if
the lines of my hands could chart
a map across the dough,
mold flour and water into
the crosshatchings of my life.

I do not believe in palmistry,
but I study my hands for promises
when no one is around.
I do not believe in magic,
but I probe the dough
for signs of life, willing
it to rise, to take shape,
to feed me. I do not believe
in palmistry, in magic, but
something happens in kneading
dough or massaging flesh;
an imprint of the hand remains
on the bodies we have touched.

This is the lifeline—
the etched path from hand
to grain to earth, the transmutation
of the elements through touch
marking the miracles
on which we unwillingly depend.

Praised be thou, eternal God,
who brings forth bread from the earth.

Boundaries

The universe does not
revolve around you.
The stars and planets spinning
through the ballroom of space
dance with one another
quite outside of your small life.
You cannot hold gravity
or seasons; even air and water
inevitably evade your grasp.
Why not, then, let go?

You could move through time
like a shark through water,
neither restless nor ceasing,
absorbed in and absorbing
the native element.
Why pretend you can do otherwise?
The world comes in at every pore,
mixes in your blood before
breath releases you into
the world again. Did you think
the fragile boundary of your skin
could build a wall?

Listen. Every molecule is humming
its particular pitch.
Of course you are a symphony.
Whose tune do you think
the planets are singing
as they dance?

Hawks

Surely, you too have longed for this—
to pour yourself out
on the rising circles of the air,
to ride, unthinking,
on the flesh of emptiness.

Can you claim, in your civilized life,
that you have never leaned toward
the headlong dive, the snap of bones,
the chance to be so terrible,
so free from evil, beyond choice?

The air that they are riding
is the same breath as your own.
How could you not remember?
That same swift stillness binds
your cells in balance, rushes
through the pulsing circles of your blood.

Each breath proclaims it—
the flash of feathers, the chance to rest
on such a muscled quietness,
to be in that fierce presence,
wholly wind, wholly wild.

Autumn Equinox

You may think of it
as marking the long descent,
the slide into winter's weariness.
Such moments are not easy to accept—
don't we all want to petition
some cosmic governor
to grant summer a reprieve?
But the sentence is always cast,
the scales will always tip,
whatever you might think is just.

In this brief, breath-catching
moment at the top
you may recall the slow climb of summer,
the safe, steady ticking up the tracks.
The self-possessed might even
gaze out and glimpse
the jostling fairgrounds and
the quiet that stretches beyond the fence.

Look quickly. Even now the car
tips forward and picks up speed.
As the wind in your face increases
and your stomach leaps, remember:
This is the ride you came for,
the fear and the sense of flying.
Winter won't seem long
when you slide to a halt
around the final curve.

Masks

What will you wear for Halloween?
The trees are changing faces, and the
rough chins of chestnut burrs
grimace and break to show their
sleek brown centers. The hills
have lost their mask of green and grain,
settled into a firmer geometry
of uncolored line and curve.

Which face will you say is true—
the luminous trees or the branches underneath?
The green husks of walnuts, the shell within,
or the nut curled intimately inside,
sheltered like a brain within its casing?

Be careful with what you know,
with what you think you see.
Moment by moment faces shift,
masks lift and fall again, repainted
to a different scene. It means,
the cynics say, there is no truth,
no constant to give order to the great equation.

Meanwhile, the trees, leaf by leaf,
are telling stories inevitably true:
Green. Gold. Vermillion. Brown.
The lace of veins remaining
as each cell returns to soil.

Food Chain

Give up pretending.
Everything, you know,
everything, sooner or later
gets eaten. Little fish,
big fish, no difference—
the world's mouth
is on you. Outside the personal,
it even has a certain glory.

When the mouse, in its last
short dash to the grain,
feels the great rush of wings,
in the flash before
the crushing beak descends,
it is finally, luminously, airborne.

In the broad, voiceless,
hours of the night
you have always known
the red beak of
your consummation
awaits you. The choice,
very simply, is this:
What will you give
your own beloved
bones and blood to feed?

Thanksgiving

I have been trying to read
the script cut in these hills—
a language carved in the shimmer of stubble
and the solid lines of soil, spoken
in the thud of apples falling
and the rasp of corn stalks finally bare.

The pheasants shout it with a rusty creak
as they gather in the fallen grain,
the blackbirds sing it
over their shoulders in parting,
and gold leaf illuminates the manuscript
where it is written in the trees.

Transcribed onto my human tongue
I believe it might sound like a lullaby,
or a child's prayer before bed.
Across the gathering stillness
simply this: "For all that we have received,
dear God, make us truly thankful."

Incarnation

The trees have finally
shaken off their cloak
of leaves, redrawn
themselves more sternly
against the sky. I confess
I have coveted this
casting off of flesh,
have wished myself
all line and form, all God.

I confess that I am caught
by the story of Christmas,
by the pronouncement of the Spirit
upon Mary's plain flesh.
What right did the angel
have to come to her
with the news of that
unprovided, unimaginable
birth? What right
had God to take on flesh
so out of season?

When Mary lay gasping
in water and blood
that was of her body
but not her own,
did she choose one gleaming,
antiseptic star to carry
her through the night?

The flesh has so few choices,
the angels, perhaps, none.
The trees will shake themselves
and wait for spring.
The angels, unbodied, will clutch
the night with their singing.
And Mary, like so many,
troubled and available,
will hear the word:

The power of the Most High
will overshadow you

and in her flesh, respond.

Salvation

By what are you saved? And how?
Saved like a bit of string,
tucked away in a drawer?
Saved like a child rushed from
a burning building, already
singed and coughing smoke?
Or are you salvaged
like a car part—the one good door
when the rest is wrecked?

Do you believe me when I say
you are neither salvaged nor saved,
but salved, anointed by gentle hands
where you are most tender?
Haven't you seen
the way snow curls down
like a fresh sheet, how it
covers everything, makes everything
beautiful, without exception?

Blessing the Candles

*Baruch atah Adonai, Eloheinu melech ha'olam, asher kidshanu
b'mitzvotav v'tzivanu l'hadlik neir shel shabbat*

Here, in the last
gentle light past sunset,
at the end of the week,
in the last years of the century,
it is hard not to grasp
after the receding light.
It is hard not to wonder
what is left: two candles burning.
Insufficient light to plant
or cook or paint the kitchen—
anything purposeful, that might
claim some conviction of the future.

There is so little we create:
a few lines that take on life,
a bookcase that stands steady.
There is so little that remains,
and always someone wanting.
I could hand out quarters
on the street all day
and no one would be saved
or safe or whole.

Outside, the street lamps
are blinking on into a false
pink phosphorescent cheer,
and we are sitting silent
in the wake of the candles'
first flare. I am watching you
looking at the candles,
or the darkness in between them.

This is the blessing that we
have kindled: this particular dark.
This space between two poles
which we, who are not angels
can inhabit. If you stand facing me,
this is what you will find:
the gap between us where
our common lives take shape,
the space between us that
we reach into for love.

Outside, the royal blue is deepening
to black. The stars begin to form
their million year old light
into constellations which we,
in our demand for form and story,
have decreed. And you and I
are caught between the candles
where we cannot help but live,
in the close and infinite abundance
held between the kindling
and the dying of the light.

Praised be Thou, eternal God,
who has sanctified us with
thy commandments, and required
of us the kindling of lights.

15

Bats

Perhaps you have not loved
this miracle—the bats
on their flickering wings
ushering in the night.
Certainly these days the darkness
comes too soon, and dimness
has outlasted color. But still,
there is the way they love
what you do not desire,
the way they appear, like stars,
without arriving. There is the
way their furred bodies shimmer
above the earth like angels,
the way they hear what we
have lost. Haven't you always
longed for wings? Imagine
hanging by your toes in some
cave or tree or belfry,
how gently the darkness opens,
how the night is filled
with imperceptible singing.

Winter Into Spring

The trees, along their bare limbs,
contemplate green.
A flicker, rising, flashes rust and white
before vanishing into stillness,
and raked leaves crumble imperceptibly
to dirt.

On all sides life opens and closes
around you like a mouth.
Will you pretend you are not
caught between its teeth?

The kestrel in its swift dive
and the mouse below,
the first green shoots that
will not wait for spring
are a language constantly forming.

Quiet your pride and listen.
There—beneath the rainfall
and the ravens calling you can hear it—
the great tongue constantly enunciating
something that rings through the world
as grace.

Groundhog Day

Celebrate this unlikely oracle,
this ball of fat and fur,
whom we so mysteriously endow
with the power to predict spring.
Let's hear it for the improbable heroes who,
frightened at their own shadows,
nonetheless unwittingly work miracles.
Why shouldn't we believe
this peculiar rodent holds power
over sun and seasons in his stubby paw?
Who says that God is all grandeur and glory?

Unnoticed in the earth, worms
are busily, brainlessly, tilling the soil.
Field mice, all unthinking, have scattered
seeds that will take root and grow.
Grape hyacinths, against all reason,
have been holding up green shoots beneath the snow.
How do you think that spring arrives?
There is nothing quieter, nothing
more secret, miraculous, mundane.
Do you want to play your part
in bringing it to birth? Nothing simpler.
Find a spot not too far from the ground
and wait.

Breaking Ground

Living in the violence of spring—
living in a time
where shells are cracking
and shapes alter,
who can afford to risk
forgetting the danger,
forgetting the moment
the crocus bulb breaks ground,
never knowing whether
snow or sun or ice
awaits in warm or jagged welcome.

There is no safety in
this restless season.
Even the sheltering ground
rejects its own,
thrusting the life it held
into the untrustworthy
and insufficient care
of air and weather.

There are no choices here—
no careful path or
reasoned way,
no holding in reserve for
some more settled,
more propitious time,
but only the unconsidered
faith of the crocus
whose saffron petals echo
or demand the sun.

Lent

What will you give up for this season,
to help life along
in its curious reversals?
As if we had a choice.
As if the world were not
constantly shedding us
like feathers off a duck's back—
the ground is always
littered with our longings.

You can't help but wonder
about all the heroes,
the lives and limbs sacrificed
in their compulsion toward the good.
All those who dropped themselves
upon the earth's hard surface—
weren't they caught in pure astonishment
in the breath before they shattered?

Forget sacrifice. Nothing
is tied so firmly that the wind
won't tear it from us at last.
The question is how to remain faithful
to all the impossible,
necessary resurrections.

Tortoises

All summer they trudged
around the yard—
impenetrable, antique,
unlikely romantics living on
hibiscus flowers and bananas,
rehearsing their primitive
mysteries just beyond
the range of sight.

But at the first cold weather
they pushed aside the door
and entered, pulling themselves
inside our thicker shell
as naturally as ever.
They are sleeping in the closet,
comfortable in that masculine array,
dropped like outdated hats
casually in the corner.

Even in sleep they are resonant
with waiting. When spring comes
they will hear the low
vibrations of that seductive voice:
Arise my love, my fair one,
and come away.
And in the lure of their
first movement
even the shoes will rise.

Camas Lilies

Consider the liles of the field,
the blue banks of camas opening
into acres of sky along the road.
Would the longing to lie down
and be washed by that beauty
abate if you knew their usefulness,
how the natives ground their bulbs
for flour, how the settlers' hogs
uprooted them, grunting in gleeful
oblivion as the flowers fell?

And you—what of your rushed
and useful life? Imagine setting it all down—
papers, plans, appointments, everything—
leaving only a note: "Gone
to the fields to be lovely. Be back
when I'm through with blooming."

Even now, unneeded and uneaten,
the camas lilies gaze out above the grass
from their tender blue eyes.
Even in sleep your life will shine.
Make no mistake. Of course
your work will always matter.
Yet Solomon in all his glory
was not arrayed like one of these.

Passover

❖

"Then you shall take some of the blood, and put it on the door posts and the lintel of the houses . . . and when I see the blood, I shall pass over you, and no plague shall fall upon you to destroy you, when I smite the land of Egypt."
—*Exodus 12:7&13*

They thought they were safe
that spring night, when they daubed
the doorways with sacrificial blood.
To be sure, the angel of death
passed them over, but for what?
Forty years in the desert
without a home, without a bed,
following new laws to an unknown land.
Easier to have died in Egypt
or stayed there a slave, pretending
there was safety in the old familiar.

But the promise, from those first
naked days outside the garden,
is that there is no safety,
only the terrible blessing
of the journey. You were born
through a doorway marked in blood.
We are, all of us, passed over,
brushed in the night by terrible wings.

Ask that fierce presence,
whose imagination you hold.
God did not promise that we shall live,
but that we might, at last, glimpse the stars,
brilliant in the desert sky.

Crab Grass

We've all admired it
even as we've cursed
the matted roots, white fingers
pointing toward new frontiers,
the tangled tapestry stubbornly
weaving the world in place.

Imagine living that way.
Imagine knowing from the ground up
that you are tied to the whole,
that you are undefeatable,
that below the surface
indefinable discoveries
are always taking place.

Don't you think there are
things worth holding on to
with a thousand arms,
ten thousand gripping toes?
Aren't the undaunted
particularly blessed?

Before you deride the faithful
consider carefully
where you will put your roots.

The Mad Poet's Love Song

———❖———

I live profligately. Dispense
big words for free.
Buy books for a single phrase
and then return, like some odd
fish, again and again
to the source. I am promiscuous.
I leave books in my bed,
fall asleep clutching stories
I've only just met.
They wake me later
but never remember my name.

Mad women love this way,
and thieves, giving everything
for style, for the flash
in the mind, the pull
at the gut. Risking everything—
old loves, old views,
for the day's perfect word,
a phrase that caresses.

Don't mock me.
There is a strange fidelity
in falling asleep to the chatter
of the printed page and
waking to the morning paper.

No? Try filling
your mouth with rhymes
and spitting them slowly,
like watermelon seeds,
across the lawn. Then
come back and tell me I'm wrong.

Shoes

When Moses met God on the mountain
the first thing the Divine spoke of
was shoes. How are we to interpret this?
Where do you find God when
you have no mountain? Some say just
stand in the lowlands and call,
but you must be willing to take
whichever god might answer.

"Whoever would save his life
will lose it," said the prophet,
who was harsh, but never cold.
Once, driving across the steaming
lake, something beckoned, but I
was too impressed by the possible
to follow. Sometimes, in the
low light it haunts me. It will

share neither face nor direction.
It mutters through its hot breath
something that sounds like "shoes."
When I gave up high heels I heard
it fluttering around the window
for a month. Some nights I think
I will live into this obsession. Go
barefoot long before spring.

Some nights the voice blows in
from the Sound:
"Take off what binds you.
You are standing on holy ground."

Elephant Seals

We could have stayed,
but we had been there
all day, gazing in slowly
softening disbelief
at the great mounds of
elephant seals
moulting on the beach—

wanting to understand
their improbable bulk,
their improbable lives,
their long migration
and their implacable stillness—
the massive serenity of those
who cannot be eaten
and who will wait to eat.

But the wind was picking up.
There was no shelter,
short of crawling down
beside one of those
leathery boulders, into the
stench of their warm sand.

And so we left too soon,
before the necessary moment.
Now I will have to spend
a lifetime learning
how to be so ugly
and so loved.

Plain Flight

The air is alive with the
commonest birds: pigeons,
starlings, crashing in waves
against the ever-opening sky.
Perhaps the wind is tossing
the birds like leaves.
Perhaps the spinning flocks
make the wind.

Ignorant, earthbound, I want
to open my mouth and be filled
with flying. I want to be full
of ordinary wings, with the flow
of bodies roped together by air,
with the visible unwinding
of patterns in time.

I want my plain self magnified
by movement, expertly caught
and carried by wind. I long,
I suppose, for the glorification
of the simplest angels, to be part
of the known unfolding. To be drawn
into and drawing the design.

Open a bag and the birds will settle,
caught by crumbs or a scatter
of grain. It isn't hard to empty
the sky of magic. But tell me:
What is it that I must open
if I would empty myself
into the turning air?

Noah

Poetry is not so easy in the city.
Nature and its images
narrow to fine points,
write indecipherable
letters and refuse to speak.

The old lady next door feeds
the birds and squirrels, keeps
six cats, talks to them from
dawn to dusk in a voice like
a soprano saxophone or a lamb.

Summer days she hangs her line
with head scarves and
old lady underwear, bleats
at the birdies and sets out
water for the cats.

She is crazy, but not confused.
I have never seen her look
other than content.
Surely God loves this woman
and her small reign:

the odd ark of her house,
the pigeons continually
sent out and the cats
lying in wait for their
inevitable return.

And always her voice
across all the threatened
yards and pavements
crying: "Here! Here!"

Watermelon

You know
what summer
tastes like—the pink flesh
of a generous earth,
this rounded life
fully ripe, fully flavored.
How could you be ashamed
at the tug of desire?
The world has opened itself to you,
season after season.
What is summer's sweetness
but an invitation to respond?
There is only one way
to eat a watermelon.
Bury your face
in the wetness
of that rosy slab
and bite.

Cormorants

This is what passes
for silence in the city.
You have fallen asleep
beside the lake, oblivious
to the roar of traffic
behind the trees.
I am watching the cormorants
out on the buoys, drying
their feathers in the sun.

Wings outstretched, they
look like pictures I have seen
of the first Christians
in prayer, crucifixes set
in disorderly rows. It hurts
when I raise my arms
to imitate their posture.
It is an attitude of receptivity
that few of us can afford.

The cormorants, of course,
have no alternative.
Their primitive feathers
do not repel the water
like a duck's, and so they
wait here 'til the sun
has dried them well
enough to dive or fly.

Ancient renunciates
in their drab black, they
have no firm place
in water or in air, but only
this peculiar stance
of openness in the place between.

I confess I am perplexed,
caught somehow
between your oblivion
and the cormorants,
empty as sundials, pointing
themselves at the sky.
How can you sleep
in such a public place, amidst
the bicyclists and fishermen?
If I opened my arms,
what would let go?

"Pray always," said the saints,
wrapped like the birds
in some prehistoric grace
that I have never understood.
"Pray always." Meaning,
I suppose, your head on
my knee, the bicycles, the city
which is never silent, where we
must, nonetheless, be still.

Common Prayer

Sunday morning at the marina—
barely enough wind to keep the kites aloft,
and so we drifted to the ground
to nibble bagels, chocolate,
giant loose-skinned oranges,
random poetry, blades of grass:
sacraments and indulgences
for the first of Spring.

And in the moment before sleep
my breast against your arm
sang *Gloria*
and the soles of my feet
cried *Sanctus* to the sun.
Placing the last chocolate
in your mouth I whispered:
"This is my body, take and eat."
And we melted,
very slowly,
on the earth's tongue.

Blessing the Wine

·❁·

Baruch atah Adonai, Eloheinu melech ha'olam,
borei p'ri hagafen.

Wine, like memory, full in the cup.
What do you taste in the glass
I have poured you?
Years ago I went picking
grapes—did I ever tell you?
One hot September Sunday
my friends and I staged
bacchanalian revels among
the dust and bees and heavy vines,
watched the juice of our
labors running off the wooden press.
Some days I feel that liquid
running slowly through my veins,
unfiltered and impure, still
carrying its sediment of dust
and stems and old sunlight.

I have been storing up
these memories for you—
racked and turned and tasted them:
Grape picking, and the afternoons
spent foraging for berries
along the tracks, up to our
elbows in berry juice and scratches.

I know I have mixed
the earth's blood with my own.
Can you taste the blood
and berries? You are holding
my history against your tongue.

I want to drink with you
from the common cup.
May memory gather
the fruits of all seasons.
May our stories all linger
like wine on the tongue.

Praised be Thou, eternal God,
creator of the fruit of the vine.

Part II

The Last Good Days

Hansel and Gretel

———— ❖ ————

"Read it again!" she says,
and again we do. The same
disaster predictably reenacted
night to night. "Don't go in!"
I want to warn them, "It's a trap!"
But children rarely listen, and
storybook characters, never.
When they see that confectionary cottage
their entrance is inevitable,
like the mosquito bite you swear
you will not scratch and always do,
and always make it worse.

Each decision is invariably
a rigged game. The witch
is always ravenous and grasping,
the children neglected and naïve.
Preach all you like about conversion,
about the will to good and unending grace—
you know the witch will never
lose her taste for the sweet
resilient flesh of boys.

Night after night we stumble
into the forest of our fears,
and night after night we're duly caught.
Every morning we awake
to the same reports of mayhem and

every morning we poke forward
some narrow stick of ourselves,
hoping to get by uneaten
one more day.

But listen. Each time through
the story I've dropped
a small white stone. Others
have too—I've seen them
glowing in the moonlight,
a nightly shifting of the scene,
building a path both ragged and new.
Next time, look down. Tear your vision
from the gingerbread house.
Drop a stone.
Tell the children.

The Wall

She wakes in the night, crying.
"What's the matter?"
I am still wallowing up from sleep, and grumpy.
"Something scary."
"What's scary?"
I have tried to layer my voice with sympathy,
but even to my ears it sounds thin.
"The wall."
"Why is the wall scary?"
"It make me sad."
"Honey, go back to sleep.
There's nothing to be scared of."
This is, of course, untrue.
The icecaps are melting
under a growing hole in the sky.
By the time she is grown
the pandas and gorillas will probably be gone.
Children with no sense of purpose
carry guns to school and
most of us pretend
our pleasures have no cost.
"The wall" is as good a name
for this rift in the world as any,
and, oh, sweetie, it makes me sad too.
Even at two in the morning
she deserves a better answer.
Sometimes we need a cry
to jolt us out of sleep.
I give her the best, the only, response I know.
"I'm here, honey.
It's OK, we're all here."

Hope

Hope wakes up in her green-lit room,
stretches, tugs at her flannel nightie,
opens her limbs to the morning.

In a moment Hope will climb down,
demand cereal, contemplate
what she wants to look like today.

In a moment the day will start to unwind,
lunchbox, sandals, numbers and glue,
gathering tarnish as it goes.

In just a moment the apple will fall,
the toast will burn, the pencil break.
But for now it's enough that Hope awakes,
slipping slowly into the lap of another day.

Riddle

How do you love the world?
How do you imagine a heart of God
large enough to take in
rapists, child abusers, earth despoilers,
gay bashers, cross burners, all
the ones we hope will never
cross our paths, but do?

How do you love a two-year-old—
your two-year-old—
who screams and kicks and rages
in a tantrum of desire and despair,
whose damp head finally finds
a resting place against the pillow
of your knotted shoulder?

Knowledge

Knowledge is power.
Power corrupts.
All the ways we name in order
to own, to split, to stack
on the ordered shelf.
The moon shone more sweetly
as a virgin, untouched.
Bumble bees had more charm
back when the physicists were
still perplexed as lilies by their flight.

And yet, the sacred need to know.
Scientists, hunter-gatherers,
fill infinite baskets with mesons,
quasars, ribosomes: all the meticulous
nuts and berries of existence.
How else would we survive?
How can you live in the family of things
without at least wanting to know
the names of a few favorite uncles?
Don't you tread a little softer
knowing that gravity is simply
a gentle dip in the terrain
of space and time?

God, they say, is all-knowing,
which somehow relates to
all-powerful and all-loving.
Which somehow relates
to that original tree.
Religion and science skip
through life with linked hands.
"Tell me about antelopes," she demands
in the imperious voice of a tiny God.
"Tell me about stars."

Ritual of Safe Passage

•❈•

For Darcey and "Ruddigore"

There is no time when you are ready,
no point at which you say "Ah, today
the world and I are fit for a child."
When the angels told Sarah
she would become a mother
she laughed.
Mary told her cousin
"My soul magnifies the Lord"
but in the moment of the annunciation
her first thoughts gave a whole new
level of meaning to the phrase
"Holy shit." That's OK.
That's why God invented faith.
Motherhood is proof of
the only article of faith you need:
There is enough love.
There will always be enough love.

Even at 2am when he won't stop crying
and you begin to understand
why a parent might hold a pillow
over a tiny, screaming face
for just a few moments' peace.
Even when the only word she says
for two solid weeks is "No!"

Even when he wears studded leather
and purple hair to a funeral
or crashes the car
or runs off to follow some band
called "Death by Rats"
there will always be enough love.

For all the mothers who tore their hearts
deciding not to bear a child
or not to raise one,
may this wanted baby be a prayer.
For all the mothers through the centuries
who did not survive the trials of labor,
may this healthy mother be a prayer.
For all the babies who did not manage
to draw that first solitary breath,
may this baby's birth-wail be a prayer.

For all of us, for the world
which is wracked with labor,
which is daily cracked open,
which is always ready
for something new to be born,
may your lives be a prayer,
the only prayer that, ultimately, matters:
There is enough love.
There will always be enough love.

Mars

— ❀ —

only comes this close
every 58,000 years or so.
Once in a lifetime pales
in comparison—725 lifetimes
laid end to end like that.

You want something so rare
to have significance. So bright
a star should herald a savior,
some whiff of glory,
the dawning of a new day.

At the very least, astrology
should declare the angry red god
ruler of our warring age,
releasing us from blame
for all the carnage.

No dice. The best we can do
is smile and wave at our neighbor
on his eccentric path, thereby
feeling infinitesimally less alone
than we have in 58,000 years.

Forgiveness

Begin with something easy—
the puppy who gnawed
on your favorite shoe,
the child who broke the teacup
that belonged to your grandmother.
Mistakes without malice don't rend
the fabric of the heart.

Limber the muscles of forgiveness
by letting go of the cruel remark
your best friend made in 9th grade,
the time your ex-lover
grabbed at your love handles
as if that were funny and cute.
Water under the bridge.
Let them go.

When you have felt
the stretch and pull
at those tight places, move on.
Go for strength, endurance.
Understand your parents
did the best they could,
all things considered.
Understand your children
are doing the same.

Admit that your body,
flawed though it may be,
has given you untold pleasure,
and will give you more.
Own up to your moments
of greed, impatience, sloth,
indifference and, yes, loathing.
Pat them gently on the head
before sending them on their way.

When you come to a place
that is truly unbending,
try massage, a warm towel, a deep breath.
Of course the pain is real,
the damage to the tissue deep.
Stretch again. Breathe again.
Take the next step.

Earthworms

Imagine. The only thing that
God requires of them
is a persistent, wriggling, moving forward,
passing the earth through
the crinkled tube of their bodies
in a motion less like chewing
than like song.

Everything they encounter
goes through them,
as if sunsets, drug store clerks,
diesel fumes and sidewalks
were to move through our very centers
and emerge subtly different
for having fed us—looser somehow,
more open to the possibility of life.

They say the job of angels
is to sing to God in serried choirs.
Perhaps. But most jobs
aren't so glamorous.
Mostly the world depends upon
the silent chanting underneath our feet.
To every grain that enters: "Welcome."
To every parting mote: "Be blessed."

Mozart & Manor

You don't expect to find such a thing
on a common Chicago sidewalk—
a mobile hump of tortoise
casually navigating the cracked concrete.
Of course I know how the absurd
breaks in, shuffling the deck
of our expectations.
God is, if anything, perversely creative,
a practical joker of the first degree.
But still, a tortoise is a tortoise,
odd enough in its own reptilian context
without wandering city streets
in that determined tip-toe amble,
pretending that one could, just as easily,
be at home in this world
anywhere,
anywhere at all,
even the corner of Mozart and Manor.

Rhythm

Before speaking, singing.
Before singing, drumming.
Every musician knows that rhythm
is the foundation upon which
the whole thing rests.

The thrum of our mother's heartbeat
never quite stops echoing
in our ears. The earth sways to the
pull of the moon, while the rain
plays castanets and the ocean
strokes its brushes across and across
the shore's taut drum.

There is nothing on earth
but motion and rest,
sound and the silence in between.
The physicists will tell you
the universe began with one
Big Bang. But that's not
what keeps it going.

That's not the Indian raga,
the rock back beat, the jig-time,
slip time and the reel. Try this.
Go down to a stream—
not a stolid river, but a
fun-loving child of a creek.

Sit down on a boulder and listen.
Underneath the water's clunk and gurgle
you will hear it.

All the liveliness in the world
originates in the sound of
10,000 pebbles
tap dancing.

Sparkles

Everyone has the urge
to adornment. From the
massive antlers of the moose
to the flashing jewels of hummingbirds,
the world declares we all
are just a bit more fabulous
than we need to be.
Rhinestones, sequins, silver thread,
belts covered in jingling gold coins—
it's all cut from the same pattern
as the peacock and the bird of paradise.
Sew a thousand silver bangles on your skirt
to sparkle as you spin.
Why would you live with less?
What is life's design
if not to find a hundred ways
we might each learn
to reflect the singular light?

Oval Beach

On a sunny day,
everyone knows how to tell
where the water meets the sky—
that hint of curve affirming
that the improbable is true,
that there is no platform
off of which we can fall.

But what of when the sky lowers,
when the waters above squeeze down
toward the waters below, as if
to unmake that original separation?
What then?

What of the undeterred children
with their sandcastles, the barefoot waders,
the dog determinedly rearranging sticks?
What of them? Have they all slid back
within tasting distance of that original stew,
tumbled *tohu v'bohu* into that world
before order was invented?

No one seems to mind. The children
squeal and splash with conventional abandon,
and even the parents show no shade of alarm.
They know the world will go on.
They know that even in the outer reaches
where the dragons lurk
no one, really, ever falls off.

They know the sky will rise again.
They know that nothing could be more expected
than this collapse and re-inflation of the firmaments,
this periodic stirring of creation,
as if we lived on the breath within
some great encircling lung,
as, no doubt, we do.

Raspberry

Almost October, and there it was,
draped over the fence,
ripe as July, and as seductive—
a stranger's bit of paradise.
It wasn't mine. Perhaps
I should have left it there,
flashing like a cardinal
in the autumn light.
But, still, the world
offers itself so lavishly, as if
it will not be refused.

Sometimes I call this "grace."
Sometimes I simply taste it
as a perfect raspberry,
out of season,
savored seed by seed,
Persephone's fruit.

Ivy

Ivy has no mercy.
Along, above, amongst, through,
Whatever the preposition,
its corded vines are bent
on conquest. Imagine
Rip Van Winkle, Sleeping Beauty,
your own exhausted self,
lying down in that ropy bed.
How long before you became
one more superfluous mound,
albeit a little greener and
more vigorous than its surroundings?
But think—would it be so bad
to move through your weariness
into that irrepressible drive?
To spend eternity stretching out
to intertwine
with everything you touch?

Before Chanukah:
After the Election

After the battle is over,
after those still standing come
limping home with the blood of comrades
in rust tattoos across their arms,

After the battle, while
the looting still continues through
the blackened streets, and statues of
false gods are erected in the town square,

Hidden in a corner
behind the stove, a child sleeps
with her head on a dog, two chests
rising in rhythm, the faint fire glow reflected
in the dog's eye defining, for the moment,
sufficient light to go on.

Annunciation to the Shepherds

It's hard not to laugh.
What a picture it makes—
the dumbfounded shepherds
and the stricken sheep,
the cacophony of bleating
and the barking of sheepdogs
dashing and nipping
in a vain attempt at order,
and over it all the angels
trying to make their
shimmery voices heard.
"A who? Wrapped in what?"
the shepherds holler back.
"*Where* are we supposed to go?"
Poor guys. They wanted directions,
a purpose, some sense of how
the story might end.
And all they got,
all any of us ever get,
was the sound of angels,
somewhere beyond the din,
singing "Glory, Hosanna"
across the improbable night.

The Camels Speak

Of course they never consulted us.
They were wise men, kings, star-readers,
and we merely transportation.
They simply loaded us with gifts
and turned us toward the star.
I ask you, what would a king know
of choosing presents for a child?
Had they ever even seen a baby
born to such simple folks,
so naked of pretension,
so open to the wind?
What would such a child care
for perfumes and gold? Far better
to have asked one born in the desert,
tested by wind and sand. We saw
what he would need: the gift
of perseverance, of continuing on the hard way,
making do with what there is,
living on what you have inside.
The gift of holding up under a burden,
of lifting another with grace, of kneeling
to acccept the weight of what you must bear.
Our footsteps could have rocked him
with the rhythm of the road,
shown him comfort in a harsh land,
the dignity of continually moving forward.
But the wise men were not
wise enough to ask. They simply

left their trinkets and admired
the rustic view. Before you knew it
we were turned again toward home,
carrying men only half-willing
to be amazed. But never mind.
We saw the baby, felt him reach
for the bright tassels of our gear.
We desert amblers have our ways
of seeing what you chatterers must miss.
That child at heart knows something
about following a star. Our gifts are given.
Have no doubt. His life will bear
the print of who we are.

Revelers

Call it a spare time—
dark afternoons
and the bones of trees
rattling against the sky.
We could use more hope,
or reason for hope. The sea
is rising, and bombs are planted
in the marketplace. It might
be better to just go to bed.
It might be better to
turn out the lights and wait
for the end to come.

The only other choice
is to dance. That and to sing
sturdy songs that have held up
across the winters,
drink wine the red of blood
that has not been shed,
feast, tell tales of heroes who
strode or stumbled through
their own bleak times.

When in doubt, revel in the darkness.
Each act of celebration is a spark.
Gathered together
they call back the sun.

The Audience

It's so easy to love them—
the man conducting
from the front row balcony,
the girl in her lavender
taffeta dress and red socks,
the toddler blissfully chewing
on her tiara. All they ask
is to wander for a couple of hours
through the rooms of your imagination,
to join the family you have
so painstakingly created.

Of course
you will open the door,
turn their red plush seats
into places at the banquet table.
There may be other places
where strangers go to fall in love,
but none so magical, so safe.

In just a few moments
they will pour back onto the street,
fading into the mass of people
shopping and dining and
chatting pointlessly on their cell phones.
But think—perhaps tomorrow
the lady blocking the intersection
or piling on groceries in the express lane
will still be clutching some small stone
gathered from your fantasy garden.
Be gentle.

Rock Garden

Who knows how long
it has been hunched down
in its corner, lurking
beneath the sludge and dead ivy,
the broken bits of toys
dropped by children we never met.
We will never know
whether this pile of stones
was carted here
to fill in a disused well,
or marks the grave
of some long-ago dog,
or whether each stone carries a memory
from some family's beach vacation
or camping trip. Some things
are permanently hidden from our sight.
But not this gathering of stones,
which only required a shovel, some gloves,
a couple of determined afternoons,
to prove that even the least attractive
corner of your life could still reveal
hidden delights, that in each of us
lie buried stones that might,
across the decades,
rise and sing.

The Fence

Something there is that doesn't love a wall,
But what about a fence—
low, picket, peeling,
and intertwined with jasmine?
Would it help if there were space
between the slats wide enough
for a fat cat to squeeze through?
And doesn't all the best complexity
happen at such borders?
Whatever you think you know
about who you have fenced in
or out is almost certainly
wrong. Just ask the cat,
the jasmine, the irrepressible ivy
and the undaunted grass.

Puppy

What would it be like
to live this way—
with such an active innocence,
so thoroughly wrapped-round with hope?
Even children lose the ability
to dance with such playful purpose
as these scuffling paws.

On good days I imagine
that God loves like this,
each encounter an uncontainable
wrenching of joy. Such an act
defies responsibility and taste.
It makes a mockery
of newspapers and calendars,
declares bills and paychecks equal
in their delightful ripping
and flat taste against the tongue.

For just a moment, stand still:
eyes wide, ears forward, nose
to the wind. Know that
dinner is provided, and a kind hand
moving toward your neck.
There. Now. Can't you feel it?
That stray breeze started
as your tail began to wag.

Rollercoaster

—⁕—

This is the finest ride—
swooping like swallows, restored
to the flight we always knew
should have been ours.
Who doesn't yearn for the
sweet hanging moment before
the long drop, the climax when
the impossible explodes
into the stunningly real?
What is better than
the perverse security of the banked turns,
knowing the danger is—probably—
all illusion?

But one ride, we know, is better.
There is nothing so sweet
as the prolonged pleasure
of the steam train ticking off
the endless fidelity of parallel tracks,
at every crossing announcing
with triumphant whistle
the simple, enduring fact
that we are here.

Center Street

He would be a part of the landscape,
if only undistinguished, semi-urban streets
had landscape—a man
more old than middle-aged,
his bowler hat and plaid shirt
dated but not unclean,
moving at a steady shuffle past
Cloteal's Beauty Shop and the Fruit Mart.

It is all so unremarkable—
not like the Santa with a shopping cart
who shares these sidewalks.
This man is plain: like his pants,
tobacco-brown, and also creased.
What calls me to him is the way he goes,
one hand held out as if in benediction,
an open palm beside his head.

Perhaps he is afraid of running into things.
Perhaps his elbow just won't straighten.
Perhaps this is the way he prays,
ambling down Center St.,
scattering blessings
across the ordinary day.

Proficiency

It takes 10,000 hours, they say,
to become a virtuoso.
10,000 hours of scales,
of drills, of stretching
toward the details of a dream.
10,000 hours of honing
the muscles to their
finest fibers, until mastery
becomes a native language,
engraved below thinking,
instinctive as your own
heart's rhythm.
10,000 hours.
Which explains why my hand
finds yours so perfectly,
interlacing so exactly,
even in sleep.

Quilting

—•❀•—

For Molly

I am stitching yellow and purple butterflies,
hour after hour of deliberate, unnecessary work.
I wish I could quilt in music,
or the bright conversation of goldfinches,
even the snare rattle of rain.
But the background of my handiwork
is incessant news of war.
They say that they can shoot a missile
from thirty miles away, and hit
within three inches of their target.

When we were both young
your father taught me the difference
between *accurate* and *precise*.
Accurate means true, conforming
to the way things really are.
Precise is merely a pinpoint,
a number followed by its contrail of digits,
defining down to the narrowest of terms.

Missiles are precise. My stitching
is accurate—if not to the pattern on the fabric,
then to the truth of butterflies themselves,
and the declaration of your new life.
There is always a different world waiting.
Patience and diligence are key.

Moses

It would have been
an ordinary day. One we might,
with the eyes of our
frantic world, call peaceful.
The light ringing of the
belled herd, a hawk's cry
sharp through the dry air —
just another bead in the long
string of days. Except. There.
A blaze that neither spreads
nor diminishes, a desert shrub
transformed into pure passion.
What will you say when
that absolute intensity calls
your name? Your language
may be different from that
long-ago shepherd, but there
is only one possible response.
When that voice calls,
you will say what Moses
so simply declared.
"Hineni" "Here I am."

Yo-Yo Ma at the Inauguration

He has to be cold, on the marble iceberg
of those steps, but how could he wear gloves
to touch the lover between his knees?
There is intimacy in sacrifice,
as much as the other way round.
He is beaming—at us, at the day,
at the colleagues who are weaving
through this shared dream. He turns to each
of them: the disabled Jew, the black man,
the brown woman, each of them a genius,
each letting our collective light shine.

This is how we do it, make real the promise
of the day. Letting the love pour through
our fingertips, our arms, our craft.
Gloves off, eye to eye,
giving full measure,
listening
with all the warm intensity
of that wide soul.

Your House

Your house has 1,000 rooms.
Every closet, drawer, cupboard,
box and bin opens up
onto another world.
You might think that
after half a century
you would have dusted
every familiar corner,
but look! The medicine cabinet
swings open on a garden
in France. Beneath the kitchen
table an African safari
sends antelope racing
over your slippered feet.
The spare room closet
contains worlds known only
to the imagination.
So many years
have already passed.
There is only time left
to explore.

Sewing

This is the power God wants:
to bind together, to stay
the raveling edge, to create
from whole cloth something
new, beautiful, warm.

The power to alter what puckers
and sags, let out the places that bind.
The power to see in the pattern
the finished whole, to cut and stitch
the vision into tangible life.

Across the world in attics and garages,
spare bedrooms and sweat shops,
a phalanx of angels sits,
needles moving steadily,
mending the fabric of the world.

The Last Good Days

What will you do
with the last good days?
Before the seas rise and the skies close in,
before the terrible bill
for all our thoughtless wanting
finally comes due?

What will you do
with the last fresh morning,
filled with the watermelon scent
of cut grass and the insistent
bird calling *sweet sweet*
across the shining day?

Crops are dying, economies failing,
men crazy with the lust for power and fame
are shooting up movie theaters and
engineering the profits of banks.
It is entirely possible
it only gets worse from here.

How can you leave your heart
open to such a vast, pervasive sadness?
How can you close your eyes
to the riot of joy and beauty
that remains?

The solutions, if there are any
to be had, are complex, detailed,
demanding. The answers
are immediate and small.

Wake up. Give thanks. Sing.

27694888R00055

Made in the USA
Lexington, KY
19 November 2013